CANBERRA

AUSTRALIAN CAPITAL TERRITORY

Canberra is Australia's largest inland city, with a population of 325 000. It was conceived, planned and constructed to be the official capital of Australia. Here Australian architecture, landscapes, customs and lifestyles mingle easily with those of other nations. Founded in 1913, Canberra lies on undulating limestone plains beneath the north-eastern slopes of the Australian Alps on the ancient lands of the Ngunnawal Aboriginal people. The name Canberra comes from an Aboriginal word and means "a meeting place". Indeed, the world's citizens come together here at scientific centres, prominent universities, the embassies and federal government offices. This cosmopolitan city hosts a lively social scene revolving around its casino, the diplomatic corps, clubs and restaurants. It also offers a multitude of delightful waterside settings for social gatherings and recreational pursuits. Fine food is found in more than 300 restaurants, cafés and bars, and over 30 wineries are within easy reach of the city.

The heart of Canberra is located in the Parliamentary Triangle on the shores of Lake Burley Griffin. An excellent network of roads and bikeways radiate from this political hub to leafy suburban enclaves that cluster around regional town centres. This is in keeping with architect Walter Burley Griffin's vision. He planned a city with plenty of public space in which it was possible to achieve "directness and speed in communication between all points". Locals are proud of their lovely city with its broad thoroughfares and wide spaces. Visitors, whether for work or pleasure, enjoy exploring and learning about Australia's past, present and future.

Steve Parish™
PUBLISHING

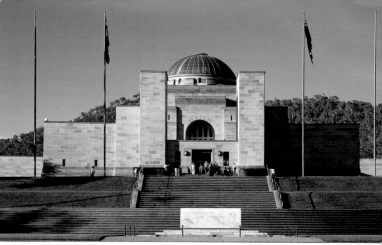

Previous pages: An aerial view across Canberra city and Lake Burley Griffin. Top, left to right: The Carillon, a bell tower on Aspen Island in Lake Burley Griffin; the Australian War Memorial at the foot of Mount Ainslie. Above: Parliament House, opened in 1988, sits above Old Parliament House. Below, left to right: Tidbinbilla Nature Reserve, 40 kilometres south-west of Canberra; sunset over the Canberra hills; Canberra Deep Space Communication Complex, Tidbinbilla Valley.

The Commonwealth of Australia came into being on 1 January 1901 with the federation of the States. The Australian Capital Territory was established in 1911 with some 2500 square kilometres of land relinquished by New South Wales. This land was on the rolling plains surrounding the Molonglo River, between Sydney and Melbourne. Yarralumla, Duntroon and Lanyon were all early homesteads. Mountain ranges, bush and national parks surround the ACT.

Canberra lies 150 kilometres inland and 571 metres above sea level, at the northern end of the ACT. This is a city in a park, the green spaces dominated by plantings of native and exotic trees, while the Australian bush is an easy drive away. Canberra's surrounds also offer wineries, historic settlements, beautiful coastal resorts, Namadgi National Park and, to the south, the glories of Kosciuszko National Park, which covers large areas of the Australian Alps.

Top, left to right: *Detail in the National Museum of Australia courtyard; autumn leaves; inside St John the Baptist Anglican Church (1845), the ACT's oldest building; tulips herald the Floriade festival.* **Above:** *Duntroon House, Royal Military College, named after the former property on which it stands. Australia's acclaimed academy opened in 1911.*

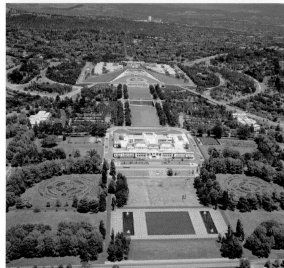

Top: *Aerial view of Capital Hill and Parliament House.* Above, left to right: *The old and the new houses of parliament; Parliament House on Capital Hill with Lake Burley Griffin in the background.*

CANBERRA, THE NATION'S CAPITAL

In 1911 an international competition to design the federal capital was announced. This was won by Walter Burley Griffin, a landscape architect from Chicago, whose aim was to combine landscape and buildings. The creation of Canberra as the nation's capital was a compromise to resolve the rivalry between Sydney and Melbourne. With a birth date of 1913, this is a young city and one of the world's few purpose-built ones. The city's centrepiece is Lake Burley Griffin, created in 1966. As the political and administrative capital of Australia, Canberra is where State and Territory members of the House of Representatives and senators meet. It has become the seat of the nation's history, learning and research. Its extensive gardens and parks fulfil Griffin's plans, while the many Commonwealth buildings are presided over by the magnificence of Parliament House. Canberra offers innovative venues such as the National Museum of Australia, opened in 2001, and Australia's European history is recorded and preserved in the remaining pioneer buildings and the Australian War Memorial.

Top to bottom: *Capital Hill by night; aerial view of Canberra city; Old Parliament House.*

Following pages: *Large areas of Parliament House are open to the public, whether parliament is sitting or not. Canberra belongs to the people of Australia.*

AUSTRALIA'S PARLIAMENT HOUSE

Opened in 1988, Australia's bicentennial year, Parliament House stands on Capital Hill. It is the home of Australia's federal government. The curved granite walls embrace 4500 rooms surmounted by an 81-metre stainless steel flagpole flying a huge Australian flag. The building, a showcase of Australian stone and timber, took a workforce of 10 000 more than eight years to complete. The Parliament House Art Collection of more than 4000 works illustrates Australia's past, present and future.

The House is open every day except Christmas, and two million people visit each year to admire the work of Australian artists and crafts people, and to observe parliamentary sessions.

Old Parliament House was opened in 1927. This gracious heritage building is now Australia's first museum dedicated to encourage people to understand Australia's democracy.

Top, left to right: *Old Parliament House is now the Museum of Australian Democracy; looking over Old Parliament House down Anzac Parade to the Australian War Memorial.* Above: *The Forecourt of Parliament House features a 100 000 piece granite mosaic designed by Indigenous artist Michael Jagamara Nelson.*

Top, left to right: *The Great Hall is panelled with fine Australian timber complemented by a bush landscape tapestry based on an Arthur Boyd painting and woven by the Victorian Tapestry Workshop; the Senate Chamber, overlooked by the public gallery.* Above: *View through the Great Verandah.* Below, left to right: *48 grey-green marble-clad pillars inside the foyer evoke a eucalypt forest; the Main Committee Room features Red Ochre Cove by Mandy Moore; airy spaciousness characterises the building.*

Top, left to right: *Courtyard of the National Museum of Australia with the Garden of Australian Dreams; detail of part of the building's exterior.*
Above: *A hot-air balloon drifts above Lake Burley Griffin and the museum.* Below: *National Museum of Australia.*

A WORLD OF DISCOVERY

The National Museum of Australia, which opened in 2001, offers a unique opportunity to explore what it means to be Australian. The museum's themes concentrate on Australia's past and future. Its exhibits, multimedia live performances and hands-on activities appeal to the child in us all. The collection includes everything from a stuffed Thylacine, the extinct Tasmanian Tiger, to convict clothing and the country's largest collection of bark paintings. Children can play in cubby houses from different parts of Australia or listen to stories inside a Boab tree. Their imaginations can be further stimulated by playing dress-ups in the Australian War Memorial's Discovery Room.

At Questacon, science and technology are combined to guide visitors on a fascinating journey of discovery. Exciting hands-on exhibits (including artificial earthquakes and caged lightning strikes) bring the physical world and its natural phenomena within grasp of enquiring minds.

Top, far left and far right: *Sculptures in the gardens of Questacon.* Top, centre left and right: *Fun and learning go hand-in-hand.* Above: *Questacon, the National Science and Technology Centre, Parkes.*

Above, clockwise from top: *Living exhibits at the National Zoo and Aquarium — Cottontop Tamarins; Boa Constrictor; Common Lionfish; Bengal Tiger.*

WILD CANBERRA

With so many famous attractions on hand, visiting families may have trouble deciding what to see in the national capital. One of the best options is a day at the National Zoo and Aquarium. Situated on 10 hectares of land (only five minutes from the heart of Canberra), this thoughtfully designed animal house enthralls both children and adults.

As Australia's only combined zoo and aquarium, this sanctuary protects some truly magnificent specimens of exotic and native wildlife. The zoo's range of big cats is a definite highlight and includes a Tigon (a lion–tiger hybrid), Serval, Snow Leopard and extremely rare King Cheetah. The aquarium features inland Australia's largest saltwater tank and showcases a hypnotic selection of marine and freshwater species. Kids will love the ZooVenture tour — an unforgettable hands-on experience that brings visitors into close contact with the zoo's captivating creatures.

THINGS TO DO IN CANBERRA

Both spectators and players can find plenty to do in Canberra, from football in winter to tennis and cricket in summer. Some are addicted to snow sports, while Rugby fans flock to barrack for the Brumbies or the Canberra Raiders. Play of a different sort is found at Casino Canberra.

Red Hill Lookout, south of the city centre, provides a great view of the nation's capital. The autumn hues of deciduous trees in the suburbs are spectacular when seen from above. You can walk, cycle or drive up Mount Ainslie to see Walter Burley Griffin's vision for Canberra realised. Springtime brings beautiful wildflowers while fruit trees blossom in Barton's Bowen Park.

Children will love a ride on the miniature steam train at Cockington Green and a stroll through this magical world of miniature buildings and gardens.

Top: *The view of Canberra and Parliament House from Red Hill Lookout.*
Above: *Casino Canberra is in the centre of the city.*

Top: *Completed in 2008, the National Portrait Gallery's new home lies in the Parliamentary Triangle.*
Above: *Portraits line the walls of the Members' Hall inside Parliament House.*

GALLERIES

Galleries in Canberra hold examples of the world's best art from bygone years to the present day. The National Gallery of Australia, which opened in 1982, contains more than 100 000 pieces including Jackson Pollock's *Blue Poles* and works by Pablo Picasso and Andy Warhol. Three levels of spacious well-lit galleries display paintings by Australian and international artists to great effect. The outdoor Sculpture Garden is a great place in which to relax and appreciate the artworks in their setting among the native plants.

Famous Australians are featured in the National Portrait Gallery, while Parliament House displays its art collection throughout its courtyards and corridors. Paintings from Sir Sidney Nolan's *Kelly* series hang in the Nolan Gallery near Lanyon Homestead. The National Museum of Australia contains a large Indigenous art collection. Canberra also has many commercial art galleries.

Above: *The National Gallery of Australia.* Below, left to right: *Gaston Lachaise's* Floating Figure; *George Baldessin's* Pear — version number 2; *Bert Flugelman's* Cones *Sculptures on display in the Sculpture Garden in the grounds of the gallery.*

Above: *Balloons glide past the National Library of Australia.*
Below, from left to right: *The High Court of Australia; the Australian National University.*

FINANCE, LAW AND LEARNING

The Holey Dollar and the Dump were Australia's first coins – both were created by punching out the centre of Spanish dollars. Since opening in 1965, the Royal Australian Mint has manufactured more than 11 billion circulating coins, having the capacity to produce two million every day. There are coin displays dating back to the First Fleet and you can mint your own coin on the guided tour.

The public can attend sittings of the High Court of Australia in a grand concrete and glass structure on the shore of Lake Burley Griffin. The seat of our highest court contains three courtrooms and a seven-storey public hall.

The National Library of Australia is a delight for readers, historians and art lovers. It holds over three million books, and newspapers, journals, maps, photographs, oral history recordings and films. Significant art works include paintings by Tom Roberts, John Glover, and a Henry Moore sculpture.

Top, left and right: *The Treasury Building at Parkes, by night and by day.*
Above: *Inside the Royal Australian Mint in the suburb of Deakin.*

Above: *Commonwealth Place.*
Below, clockwise from top left: *Malaysian High Commission; Embassy of Spain; Irish Embassy; Thai Embassy.*

Above: *The tile-roofed miniature city that is the Chinese Embassy.*

INTERNATIONAL CANBERRA

England appointed her first High Commissioner to Australia in 1936, starting Canberra's diplomatic corps. The first non-Commonwealth country to establish permanent diplomatic representation was the United States of America, which built its embassy of sandstone brick in the early 1940s.

A drive around Canberra's suburbs of Red Hill and Yarralumla reveals the variety of embassies and high commissions. Many of the buildings have been designed to evoke the traditional housing of the nations they represent on the foreign soil of Australia. The range of styles gives Canberra's architecture an international flavour. Traditional Balinese statues line the steps of the Indonesian Embassy, while the Greek Embassy features Parthenon-like marble-clad colonnades. The Embassy of the United States of America resembles an eighteenth-century Virginian mansion, while Papua New Guinea's embassy is a replica of a Sepik River spirit-house. Two marble lions guard the Chinese Embassy with its magnificent tiled, upcurved roofs; colourful metal cattle graze on the grass by the New Zealand High Commission. There are close to 90 diplomatic missions in Canberra. Several times each year, notably during Floriade, some embassies hold open days and are eagerly inspected by the public. The diplomatic staff and their families enrich Canberra's cosmopolitan character.

Top: *A diorama of the Charge of the Light Horse at the Wells of Beersheba, World War 1.*
Above, left to right: *Australian Vietnam Forces National Memorial; Rats of Tobruk Memorial and the Eternal Flame;*
New Zealand Memorial.

LEST WE FORGET

The Australian War Memorial was conceived by Charles Bean, Australia's Official Historian of the First World War, as a tribute to the Australians who had lost their lives in the Great War of 1914–18. The imposing sandstone building with its copper-sheathed dome stands at the foot of Mount Ainslie among lawns and eucalypts at the head of Anzac Parade, a wide ceremonial avenue bordered by monuments to the Australian Armed Services. The commemorative Roll of Honour lists the names of more than 102 000 men and women who died serving their country in war since 1885. Significant war relics, such as a Lancaster Bomber and the remains of a Japanese midget submarine that was captured in Sydney Harbour in 1942, are displayed in exhibition galleries.

Almost one million people visit the Memorial, one of the world's great national monuments, each year. National Anzac Day and Remembrance Day ceremonies are held here annually.

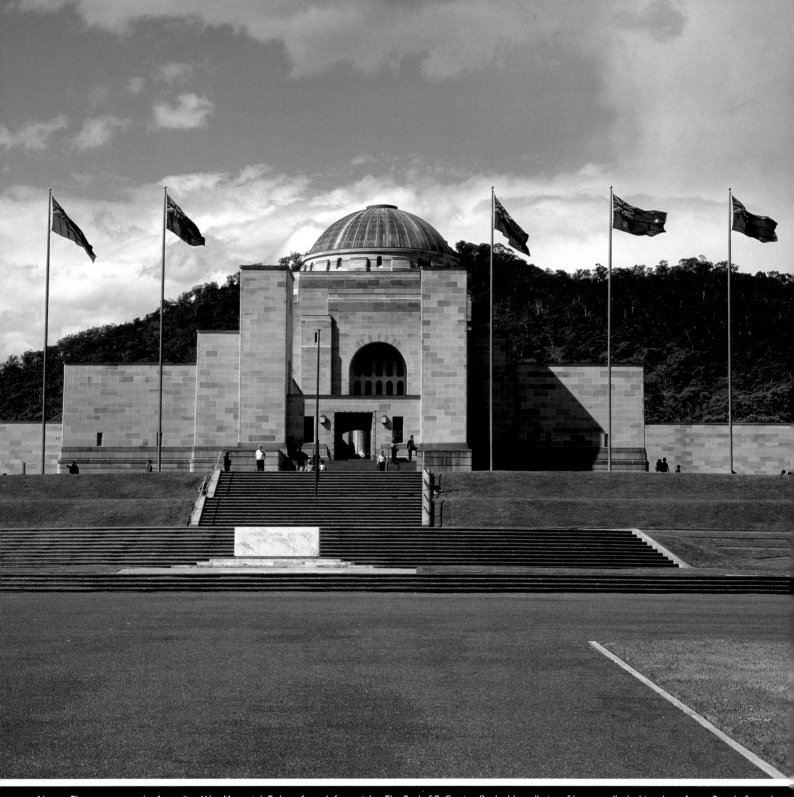

Above: The entrance to the Australian War Memorial. Below, from left to right: The Pool of Reflection flanked by galleries of honour rolls; looking down Anzac Parade from the Australian War Memorial to Parliament House across Lake Burley Griffin.

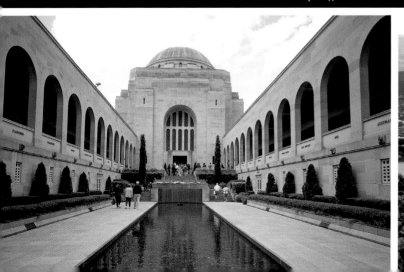

PARKS AND GARDENS

Canberra's colour and beauty are reflected in its four seasons: delicate spring blossom, flamboyant summer blooms, russet autumn leaves and winter snow-capped mountains. The many parks and public gardens provide plenty of open space with lawns, trees, flowers and excellent amenities.

Sculptures and tranquil ponds fringe the walks of Commonwealth Park. Historic rose gardens grace Old Parliament House, surrounding its public tennis courts, cricket pitch and bowling green. Covering 90 hectares on the lower eastern slopes of Black Mountain, the Australian National Botanic Gardens contain more than 5500 species, the world's finest display of Australian flora. The themed gardens simulate classic Australian habitats such as mallee scrub, and a misty rainforest attracts beautiful birds. The Cotter Reserve, by the Murrumbidgee and Cotter Rivers junction, is a popular picnic spot. Lennox Gardens, on the shores of Lake Burley Griffin, contain a peaceful Japanese garden.

Top: *Brightly coloured spring tulips.*
Above: *The magnificent landscaped gardens of Commonwealth Park.*

Top, left and right: *Cockington Green features miniature buildings from around the world together with tiny gardens.* Above: *The Australian National Botanic Gardens contain 90 000 plants from 5500 Australian species.* Below, left to right: *Colours of The Australian National Botanic Gardens.* Following pages: *A view across Lake Burley Griffin.*

Top, left to right: *Old Parliament House and Parliament House on the shore of Lake Burley Griffin.* Above: *The National Capital Exhibition at Regatta Point tells how Canberra was named, designed and built.* Below, left to right: *Scenes around Lake Burley Griffin.*

Top: *Sailing on Lake Burley Griffin.* Above, left to right: *Boat trip past Captain Cook Memorial Water Jet; walkers and joggers on the lake's foreshore pass many notable buildings, such as the National Library.*

ENJOYING LAKE BURLEY GRIFFIN

Lake Burley Griffin, Canberra's centrepiece, was formed in the 1960s by damming the Molonglo River. It is 11 kilometres long with 35 kilometres of meandering landscaped shoreline. The lake's calm waters are used as a playground all year round. Popular activities include sailing, windsurfing, rowing, swimming and fishing. There are picnic, barbecue and scenic areas as well as walking tracks and cycleways. For family fun, hire a tandem bike or a paddle boat. One of the best ways to see the whole lake is on a cruise.

Canberra's business and commercial centre, Civic, sits on the lake's north shore with Parliamentary Triangle on the south. On Aspen Island stands the National Carillon. When it is operating, the Captain Cook Memorial Water Jet, off Regatta Point, sends a plume of water almost 150 metres into the air at a speed of 260 kilometres per hour. On the lake's shore, the Captain Cook Terrestrial Globe tracks the British navigator's Pacific voyages.

Top, left to right: *The Canberra Centre in Civic, the city's commercial heart.* Above: *Belconnen shopping centre offers high-quality goods from all over the world, as do Canberra's other suburban centres.*

COFFEE AND RETAIL

Unlike most large cities, Canberra developed in harmony with the demands and benefits of motor vehicles. It has excellent roads and its suburbs are decentralised and within easy reach of major shopping centres, such as those at Woden, Tuggeranong and Belconnen. Civic, Canberra's commercial centre, stands on the north shore of Lake Burley Griffin and features fine shops, superb theatres and world-class restaurants. Smaller boutiques with elegant jewellery and designer labels can be found at Kingston and Manuka; stylish Australian fashions are seen at Lonsdale Street in Braddon.

For the handmade and the home-produced, the markets stock everything from art and craft to books, clothing, toys, cakes, cheese and fresh coffee. The Old Bus Depot Markets are a treasure trove for many each Sunday. Saturday morning's Regional Growers Market in the Kuringai Building in Exhibition Park is the largest of its type in the Southern Tablelands.

Above: *The Old Bus Depot Markets in Kingston are a favourite destination on Sundays.*
Below: *Outdoor pleasures at the city cafés of Northbourne Avenue.*

AUSTRALIAN INSTITUTE OF SPORT

Australia has always been a sporting nation: sport is a vital part of our life and culture. Catch up on the action in Canberra with Rugby Union and Rugby League, Aussie Rules, tennis, cricket and golf. January's Canberra Women's Classic is part of the lead-up to the Australian Tennis Open and the Prime Minister's XI cricket match is a popular event at Manuka Oval.

Established by the Federal Government in 1981, the Australian Institute of Sport is home to some of our present and future Olympians. They train here using the latest resources in sports science and medicine. Many of the facilities are open to the public, including tennis and basketball courts, indoor swimming pools, spa, sauna and athletic tracks. You can tour the complex with an elite athlete and test your skill at virtual golf, rowing or some other popular sport in the interactive Sportex exhibition, complete with sporting memorabilia.

Above: *The grounds of the Australian Institute of Sport at Bruce feature bronze sculptures of athletes.*

Above, left to right: *The main entrance to the Australian Sports Commission, which coordinates the government's contribution to sport; Australian Institute of Sport sculpture.*
Below: *Aerial view of the Australian Institute of Sport at Bruce.*

Top and above: *Colour bubbles over Canberra as hot-air balloons take to the skies.*

BLOOMS AND BALLOONS

Canberra's temperate climate is wonderful for gardens. Each spring, the ACT celebrates Floriade – Australia's largest flower festival. City streets and parklands blaze with colour as more than one million bulbs, annuals and blossom trees flower together. The Open Gardens Scheme allows the public to enjoy dazzling private gardens. The massed floral displays at Commonwealth Park make an enchanting setting for the outdoor entertainments and cultural events of Floriade.

One of the most delightful ways to see the city is from a balloon. Gently floating over Canberra is an exhilarating experience. Regular champagne flights take off at dawn to give a bird's eye view of Canberra's planned layout. The founding of the national capital is celebrated with a ten-day festival each March. During the festival, some 50 novelty balloons from Australia and overseas rise from the parliamentary foreshore and glide over the city.

Above: *Floriade, the festival of flowers, spreads a carpet of blooms over Canberra's green spaces.*

Below: *Tulips, daffodils, hyacinth and other lovely bulbs feature in Floriade's lush display at Commonwealth Park each September and October.*

Top: *Yarralumla, the Governor-General's residence.* Above: *Duntroon House, now the officers' mess at Royal Military College.*
Below, from left to right: *Interior view of the stained glass windows and exterior of St John the Baptist Anglican Church, consecrated in 1845.*

HISTORY

There are many places of historical interest in and around Canberra, as the region has a rich indigenous and farming heritage. Pioneer Robert Campbell built Duntroon House, now part of the Royal Military College, in 1853, and he built Blundell's Cottage for his ploughman five years later. The cottage is named for its second tenants, George and Flora Blundell, who lived there from 1874 to 1933. Lovingly restored, the cottage features artefacts and relics from the nineteenth century. Lanyon Homestead is a grazing property from the same era. Within its borders stands a gum tree from which Aborigines stripped bark to fashion a canoe. Gracious old churches include those of St John the Baptist in Reid, and All Saints Church, a former railway station, at Ainslie. Set in sweeping landscaped grounds, Yarralumla was previously an early pioneering family's homestead. Calthorpe's House at Red Hill, built in 1927, provides a glimpse into the more recent past.

Top: *Glimpses of Canberra's history reflected in its buildings.*
Above: *Blundell's Cottage, built in 1858 by Robert Campbell.*

Top, left to right: *Eastern Grey Kangaroo with joey; long-legged, flightless Emus have soft, shaggy grey-brown feathers.*
Below, left to right: *The solitary, tree-dwelling Koala; the sociable and constantly active Sulphur-crested Cockatoo.*

Top: *Juvenile Common Wombat.* Above, left to right: *The Corroboree Frog lives in moss beds high in the Australian Alps; the mouse-sized, nectar-eating Eastern Pygmy-possum.*

NATURAL HISTORY

The fruit and berry-bearing trees in the green spaces in and around Canberra make ideal bird habitat. Koalas may be seen in stands of eucalypt trees in bush near the city. Canberra is called the "Bush Capital" because of the 30 bushland settings that make up Canberra Nature Park. In certain areas mountain bikes and horse riding are permitted.

Almost half of the Australian Capital Territory is set aside as national park and nature reserve, which offer countless opportunities for outdoor recreation and encounters with Australian wildlife.

Close at hand are the placid Jerrabomberra Wetlands Nature Reserve and the cascading waters of the Murrumbidgee River. Further afield are Tidbinbilla's native animal and waterbird enclosures, and the tranquillity of Namadgi's remote mountain peaks. Namadgi National Park is home to Possums, Platypuses and the Gang-gang Cockatoo, bird emblem of the ACT.

THE NATIONAL CARILLON

The British Government gave Canberra a musical birthday gift, a bell tower, to mark its fiftieth anniversary in 1963. Completed in 1969, it was formally accepted by Queen Elizabeth II in 1970 on behalf of Australians.

The National Carillon rises 50 metres from Aspen Island in Lake Burley Griffin, near Kings Avenue Bridge. Its three angular columns are clad in quartz and opal chip and contain a passenger lift, a steel staircase and a service shaft. Its 55 bronze bells, weighing between seven kilograms and six tonnes, are tuned through four and a half octaves, and are best heard within a hundred-metre radius of the tower. The notes drift across Lake Burley Griffin and through Kings and Commonwealth Parks during regular recitals by local or visiting carillonists. The instrument dates back to fifteenth-century Flanders and is played by using hands and feet to strike batons, pedals and levers attached to clappers.

Top and above: *Views of the National Carillon by day and night.* Opposite: *The three-part tower of the National Carillon, seen across Lake Burley Griffin, symbolises national unity and harmony.*

Above: *Tidbinbilla Valley is the location of the Canberra Deep Space Communication Complex.*
Below, left and right: *The dishes receive signals and transmit commands from deep space, as well as tracking spacecraft.*

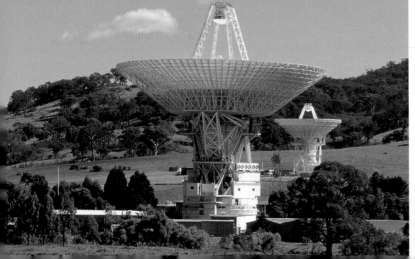

Top: *Eastern Grey Kangaroos people-watching at Tidbinbilla Nature Reserve.*
Above, left and right: *The information centre entrance.*

TIDBINBILLA

Canberra's commercial and residential areas are surrounded by bush. At Tidbinbilla Nature Reserve, 45 kilometres from the city centre, you can see mobs of Eastern Grey Kangaroos, Koalas, and flocks of waterbirds in their natural surroundings. The region is rich in indigenous and pioneer heritage and there are walking trails, picnic and barbecue facilities, and ranger-guided activities.

Tidbinbilla Valley is the site of the Canberra Deep Space Communication Complex, part of NASA's Deep Space Network, and one of only three such stations in the world. The mountain ridges reduce man-made radio-frequency interference. There are views here of the largest antennae in the southern hemisphere, including one that returned images of Neil Armstrong walking on the moon in 1969. The Canberra Space Centre is open to the public daily and visitors can discover Australia's role in space exploration. Exhibits include a 3.8 billion-year-old piece of the moon, flown space hardware and the latest images from Mars.

BLACK MOUNTAIN TOWER

Black Mountain Tower rises 195 metres above the summit of Black Mountain, from its top giving panoramic views of Canberra, its suburbs and Lake Burley Griffin. The tower houses three levels of state-of-the-art equipment that provides vital telecommunications links. The tower was chosen to join the World Federation of Great Towers in 1989. Open to the public since 1980, the tower's facilities are open every day from 9 a.m. to 10 p.m. The "Making Connections" exhibit records the history of Australian telecommunications. Diners at the revolving restaurant can delight in the ever-changing scenery as they enjoy their meals.

Black Mountain stands 812 metres above Canberra's limestone plains and bushwalking tracks span its north-western slopes. The Australian National Botanic Gardens are nearby at the end of Black Mountain Drive.

Top, left to right: *Varying moods of Black Mountain Tower.* Above: *Canberra's most conspicuous landmark rises in the distance.* Following pages: *An aerial view of Black Mountain Tower and Canberra.*
Page 48: *Different lights and seasons show the changing beauty of Canberra's parks and public buildings.*